How to B Estate Appraiser

A Step-by-Step Guide with Practical Advice & Real-World Insight for Starting Your Own Home Appraisal Business

By

Mathew Johnson

Autumn Leaf
Publishers

Design & Illustration by Jordy Roberts

First Edition

Contents

Introduction

I had been working for years as an Administration Officer at a large utility company in Dallas, Texas. Despite the experience and my extraordinary qualifications in the area, I did not feel fulfilled by the job.

Every time I would contemplate the future, on my retirement, I would feel a surge of fear. Would I be ready? Would I have enough? What will keep me busy? What will give me a constant income?

Every time I would make my calculations, they would not add up. So day and night, I kept thinking about it.

One day, as I was perusing through a business journal that I had come across at the office, I found an article that would later change my life.

"Treasure in Real Estate," read the title. This caught my attention immediately, as I had been eager to find 'treasure' that would give me lifetime returns. I read through the article, and it made me very interested in the home appraisal business.

I did extensive research on business investing and sought advice from various resources. A financial advisor gave me substantial information on investments and which had the greatest potential of growth.

You can imagine my joy when he mentioned the home appraisal industry as a promising business venture. To me, that was a green light to proceed with my entrepreneurial dreams.

Since home appraisal involves a lot of math and some statistics, I also completed training with a real estate business institute in Dallas. I gained detailed know-how on how to do home appraisals.

Registering a company and getting the required licenses was quite a hustle, but I managed to get them after making the required applications. With that, I was able to start my home appraisal company.

At first, I did it as a part-time job, but my business was booming, and I had to resign from my administrative position in April 1987.

The experience was great. I faced challenges and also reaped several successes, just like in any other business.

Over the years, the company has grown from a small business whose offices were at my home, to a large company with about twenty employees. Our income has also grown by a large scale over the years.

When I look at the business now and reminisce about where we began, I have no regrets. I know that I got into the business that was most suitable for me.

I also feel good when I see young people who have just completed college getting their start at our company and having tremendous growth in their careers. Some of our employees have become renowned home appraisers with good reputations in the industry.

I have mentored home appraisal experts who have also mentored other home appraisal agents.

Right now, I have the luxury of having retired, but my company still thrives. With responsible employees who have the desire and zeal to ensure the success of the business, I always know that my company is in good hands.

It was not easy to let go, but eventually, I found people who are trustworthy and full of integrity to ensure the smooth running of the company. I, however, go to the office from time to time to ensure that everything is working out fine and to motivate my team to build the company.

It has not always been smooth sailing, but the experience is worthwhile. For this reason, I would love to share with you the knowledge that I have gained from the experience and a few secrets that can help you be successful in this business.

What is Home Appraisal?

A home appraisal is simply an unbiased, professional evaluation of a home.

Normally, an appraiser has no interest in the sale of the property or whether you have the ability to refinance the property as a result of the value they arrive at.

Instead, he or she gets compensated on the condition that the value of the home is provided. Individuals require a home appraiser when carrying out purchase-and-sale transactions and refinance deals.

In purchase-and-sale transactions, an appraisal is used as the determining factor on whether a home's price on the contract is appropriate. To a seller, the home appraisal helps determine the value of their home. To a buyer, the appraisal makes clear a fitting price for the estate.

In refinance dealings, an appraisal guarantees the lender that it is not giving the debtor more money than the state's value. Moneylenders usually want to ensure that property holders do not borrow more money for a property as the home works as a warranty for the secured loan.

Should the borrower evade paying the mortgage or loan, the lender will trade the home as a way to recover the money it lent to the borrower. An appraisal serves as a protection tool for the bank, enabling it to protect itself from loaning out more than it may be able to recoup in worst-case scenarios.

City governments also use appraisals to determine the value of a property and levy taxes against it.

With so much riding on the appraised value of your home, it is essential to comprehend what appraisers actually look at when assessing your home.

What an Appraiser Examines

An appraiser visits your home to measure its dimensions, examine its amenities, and evaluate its overall condition. The appraisal usually only takes about 30 to 45 minutes. This is done on both the interior and exterior parts of the house.

The appraiser takes photos of the exterior, the garage, and every interior room. The documents of properties comparable to yours are then reviewed—ideally, your neighborhood's properties that have sold recently.

Based on the home assessment and the reviewed reports, the appraiser comes at a professional conclusion of the probable cost of your property in the market. This value is used by the bank—along with your assets, credit history, and income—to determine how much it will lend you.

In detail, an appraiser's interests are:

Exterior and interior condition.

Usually, a home is made up of a foundation, walls, and a roof. All three of these play significant roles in the reliability and functionality of a home. The appraiser will pay serious attention to all of them. In the assessment, the appraiser will look for flaws in the overall structure of the house, as well as any damage to these components.

Even if the roof, covering, and foundation are all in excellent shape, the interior of your home is still significant to the appraiser during the assessment. Things like walls, plumbing, windows and doors, kitchen, flooring, electrical, and bathrooms are all primary parts of a home.

The appraiser is obliged to know about all these and have the ability to tell good from the bad. You can, therefore, rest assured that he or she will look closely at your home. This is true even down to the appliances in your home and the light installations you have.

Total room count.

The scope of your property and the size of your home are both relevant factors for the appraiser. People tend to fancy more spacious, lavish homes and larger lots. You can, therefore, expect these to be high considerations when your house is under evaluation.

The more bedrooms and bathrooms in your house, the more you should anticipate your home is worth. Especially if they are spacious, convenient, and accommodating. Homebuyers like the possibility to develop and are more inclined to desire a lot that will enable this. The home's square footage will make up a substantial part of what goes into making a conclusion on the appraised value of the home.

Exterior amenities.

These include garages, decks, and porches. Simply, anything outside that makes the home more convenient and attractive.

Home improvements.

When valuing a home, the appraiser does not stop at its original construction. He or she will also pay close attention to any improvements that you have made and the quality of those improvements.

In case of a renovated bathroom or kitchen, new floor, an HVAC system, or new appliances, the appraiser will consider all of these to determine overall value.

Purchasers and moneylenders cherish the latest appliances and quality re-modeling because they add to the lasting value of the home. A kitchen renovation and new dishwasher may top up another 20 years to the lifespan of the kitchen. This is essentially good for everyone involved.

Home improvements to kitchens and bathrooms, windows, roof, and the home's systems over the previous 15 years usually make a home more up to date, functional, and livable by current standards. These improvements will unquestionably be part and parcel of how an appraiser determines the value of a residence.

Location.

Location matters! It will be a valuable factor to your appraiser.

Homes in more alluring and sought-after areas obtain more high-priced appraisals than similar homes in other areas. Generally, desirable and popular neighborhoods are those with low crime rates, lots of economic opportunities, and excellent schools.

Trends in society also play a crucial role. There are many reasons an area can experience a surge in popularity. If the local people feel that a particular neighborhood is the best place to be, then property rates there may rise.

The rise may simply be due to people's desire to be there. In the appraisal, other location features, such as the views from home and the level of privacy from neighbors, also play a vital role.

Most appraisals include a Comparative Market Analysis (CMA). The CMA uses the sale price of similar homes nearby to determine the target property's fair market value better.

Extras and additions.

The other extra things that make your home unique will also be considerations in the appraisal. A house may be very basic, or it may have some accessories that make it more appealing and alluring.

For instance, air conditioning in a colder climate may be unusual in that particular area but excellent for the homeowner during the few hot months of summer.

Another example is the swimming pool. If it is in good shape and in a place where people are willing to pay for them, it could supplement the value of your home.

You may consider things like fireplaces, a garage, a security system, or insulated windows as primary. These things can, however, add value to your home during the appraisal process.

These are all deciding factors that appraisers keenly look for during the home appraisal process.

Home Appraiser versus a Real Estate Agent

Every so often, people are confused about the role of the home appraiser and a real estate agent. Many times people imagine them to be one and the same profession, which is actually not true. These two professions are different, despite the fact that they deal in the same industry.

Let us briefly look at what the differences between a home appraiser and a real estate agent are.

Advocacy for a certain price.

Usually, getting the best listing and final sale price for their clients is every real estate agent's goal. Booking agents want to guarantee that sellers walk away with the most eminent possible sales price. They are hired to be an advocate for sellers.

Agents will frequently share information that can impact sales prices around to seller. Such information includes estate, divorces, the current purchase of another home by the seller, or the owner's relocation to a different town.

A real estate agent's perception of market value may differ from that of the appraiser when playing the role of an advocate.

Presenting an unbiased report.

Appraisers must verify that they are not advocates for any company, and compensation is not contingent on the purchase of a particular appraised value. Although they occasionally receive assignments from lenders, appraisers operate under written precepts of the Uniform Standards of Professional Appraisal Practice (USPAP). One of these rules dictates that they must remain unbiased.

Furthermore, government laws and regulations prevent appraisers and lenders from communicating in any way that would unfairly alter the appraisal. An example of such rules is the Truth in Lending Act.

These are there to safeguards homeowners by ensuring that lenders, or any other party to the transaction, cannot affect appraisal specialists to inflate or deflate the price of a home.

Another principal contrast between appraiser and real estate agent is the former has more guidelines when selecting data than the latter. These factors include the time when the properties were sold, locations of estates, the physical similarities of these homes to the appraised one, among many more.

When doing quality appraisal reviews, quality control experts apply these guidelines in determining if the comparable sales are surely appropriate and the most reliable in establishing market value. This helps them assess the reliability of an appraisal report.

Navigating appraiser/agent communication.

The same regulations that limit how appraisers talk to lenders also inhibit specific interactions amid appraisal professionals and real estate agents. In short, no communication can take place between the two in an attempt to influence his or her conclusion of value.

Nevertheless, this does not prevent agents from sharing their data on comparable sales with appraisers. Agents must, however, be cautious in how they share this information.

Many of the lenders have a process of adequately submitting supplementary data to the appraiser for deliberation. Should an agent offer reconsidered comparable sales, it is entirely up to the appraiser to decide if the comparable sales are meaningful and more related to those selected originally.

interior spaces. But, the reflection and evaluation of the appraisers and inspectors on home features are different.

Let us briefly have a look at how each of them views a property to see the difference clearly.

How home inspectors view a property.

Property inspectors' walkthroughs are often more comprehensive than those of the appraiser. These walkthroughs are detailed because inspectors ought to have a holistic representation of a home's components, its condition, and its usability.

Additionally, when it comes to taking photos and notes, inspectors may use other devices to find areas with problems. For instance, an inspector may use an infrared camera to spot areas that are prone to the growth of molds.

Typically, the job of an inspector involves determining the state of a specific property, whether it is operational, and if there is a likelihood of damages of structure or other parts in the future.

For example, a poorly rated home could flood more often, thus leading to future water damage and an increase of mold. This and other matters influence whether the house continues to be a comfortable and habitable space for the owners.

Doing home inspections gives customers complete exposure to the state of a house. It highlights all issues from the small ones to the major ones. An inspection offers this crucial information, including anything that may bring about a cost of repair that could influence the buyer.

Inspectors also give suggestions for adjustments as well as their approximate costs.

Appraisers view of a property.

Unlike the inspectors, an appraiser's walkthroughs are not as lengthy. This is because most of the investigation work takes place away from the house.

This analysis covers a survey of data on comparable sales and other investigations, like the neighborhood trends, the appeal of the school district, new construction nearby and renovations, accessibility to shopping and workplace, as well as overall habitability and demand in the market.

Like inspectors, appraisers also take photos, measurements, and notes. However, instead of having a look at whether the features of a home are in excellent or mediocre condition, appraisal professionals ascertain how the facilities influence price in the local market.

An appraiser's inspection tells of apparent issues. For instance, if the finishing of a house is falling off, the appraisers consider that fact in their reports. They are, however, likely to miss noting down faults that cannot be seen with the naked eye, like defective installation behind the walls.

Furthermore, appraisers acknowledge the functionality of a home in its community with regard to its value. Inspectors look at the property under inspection only, whereas the appraisers factor in comparative sales, other variables in the market, and nearby amenities.

Appraisals, Inspections, and Home Sales

The results of both the appraisal and home inspection may have an influence on whether the purchase of a home goes through.

Banks and mortgage underwriters need the appraisal to make a conclusion if a house is an adequate security for the mortgage proposition to the buyer. If the house is appraised for less than the offer of the buyer and pre-confirmed loan amount, the buyer must come up with the difference.

Alternatively, he or she can find a plan to withdraw from the sale or re-adjust the price of the property as per the appraisal.

An inspection of a home can additionally prompt a buyer to waive a purchase. Frequently, clients incorporate a property inspection probability in their offers.

This means that their arrangement to purchase the house at the amount offered is based on the home's condition fitting a standard that they find satisfactory.

If the property requires renovations, buyers can bargain for a lower sale price to meet the costs, or request the seller to make the necessary modifications.

Starting a Home Appraisal Business

There are many advantages to running your own home appraisal business. In your business, you have meaningful command over the working calendar and the potential of income. You also get to operate the practice in a way that fits you.

It sounds appealing, doesn't it?

Since it is appealing, the home appraisal business requires a lot of background work and study involved.

For one to begin a home appraisal business, there are a few things you need to do. Some of these things include:

- Having a definite outline of achievements you would like to accomplish

- Registering the company

- Obtaining the mandatory permits and insurance coverage

- Buying or leasing office equipment and software

When starting a home appraisal business, there are basic steps you need to take.

Pick a Niche Market

It is said by many that if you strive to do everything for everybody, then you will primarily become nobody to anyone.

This saying is true because your potential buyers will not have an idea precisely what your practice is. Thus, they will not trust you enough to grant you their business.

Before you commence taking any jobs, ensure that you pick a niche market. When doing so, consider your strengths, expertise, and the sort of properties that you enjoy appraising.

Some appraisers may pay attention to a particular subset of the real estate market. For instance, various appraisers specialize in the evaluation of the after construction value of a home project that is under construction, whereas others may concentrate on business office structures.

Nevertheless, you can base your niche on many factors besides the type of properties. It may be from a distinct set of clientele with shared attributes. For example, you could be the appraisers that divorce attorneys go to when handling cases in a divorce settlement.

Alternatively, you could concentrate on the appraisal business for homes in a particular region. Considering your already-acquired vast knowledge of these neighborhoods, the insights you have could grow into an essential competitive advantage to your customers. Additionally, your turnaround period may be a lot swifter following the abundance of knowledge and experience in where to get the research data.

Obtain the Real Estate Appraiser License

For you to begin an appraisal business, regulations assert that you need the state license to do the appraisal activities.

The kind of license you obtain usually depends on the kind of properties you decide to work with and their value. For instance, if you were to attempt your venture into industrial real estate appraising, then you need to acquire the Certified General Appraiser license.

There are four levels of appraiser licenses in many states. These are:

- Appraiser Trainee license

- Certified General Appraiser

- Licensed Residential Appraiser

- Certified Residential Appraiser

When applying for whichever of the four licenses, you will realize that each of them has its own specific requirement.

These requirements differ in work experience, appraisal courses, examinations, and college-level education qualifications. Every state has its stipulated requirements for each license, which you can find on various sites online.

I greatly encourage you to take a certified license. This is because many financial institutions and moneylenders accept appraisal reports executed by a Certified Appraiser only. It also allows you to appraise a more extensive range of real estate.

Establish a Business Entity

It is of much importance to take safety measures when it comes to individual legal responsibility, as much as we want to be successful in business.

Lots of appraisers usually form an isolated commercial entity to shield themselves from being personally answerable to court cases against their establishment. Several appraisers would register as a Limited Liability Company (LLC) or as an S-Corp or C-Corp, which are more advantageous.

Likewise, bringing a business entity into being may bring about excessive elasticity on the distribution of the business's returns, thus accruing some tax advantages. Some states would require you to register for taxes too.

Always consult with your accountant and lawyer to find out how to handle different situations in your appraisal business venture.

Open a Business Bank Account

When your appraisal business finally brings its operations into being, it is essential that you open a bank account. This bank account will be used for depositing the revenue accrued in business and making payments for the diverse expenditures.

As a businessperson, under no circumstances should you use a similar bank account for your individual and business dealings. Doing so would toughen the keeping of a track record. Also, you cannot show a valid justification of the separateness of your business entity from your private assets.

In case you want to open a business bank account, ensure that you obtain the Federal Employee Identification Number (EIN). This number can be obtained within minutes, and ought to be accessible to you as soon as you register the business entity online.

https://www.irs.gov/businesses/small-businesses-self-employed/how-to-apply-for-an-ein

I consulted several appraisers about payments and realized that some clients prefer paying the appraisal fee using a credit card. They said that this is not a good idea because it would bring about major chaos in case of a dispute. Even if only a few clienteles clash with the card company over the transactions. Many of them highly recommend that one uses either cash or cheque.

Acquire Bookkeeping Software

You will not be able to gauge the progress of your business without a clear financial record. It is crucial to have a track record of all your expenses in business, the exact dollar amounts, sources of revenue, and the specific dates that they were processed. This information is also of much importance when it comes to reporting your taxes.

If you have just started the business and hope to keep you cost low, you could use Microsoft Excel Spreadsheets, which is most accessible. You could also use software such as QuickBooks (https://quickbooks.intuit.com/) which is preferred by many business people.

Keeping records is not only done in software, but some apps could be of assistance. Some of these apps even enable you to amass copies of receipts.

This is quite handy in the auditing of your tax filing by the tax department.

Configure an Office Space

In this case, there are a vast number of options depending on your specific needs

You could rent an office which would be very beneficial when having frequent meetings with clients. It could also be beneficial if you have employees working for you. There are rental agreements that may include various amenities, like a fax machine and furniture.

Nonetheless, if you usually have occasional meetings with a handful of customers, you may well consider using a virtual office. This option is based on pay-as-you-rent.

https://www.opusvirtualoffices.com/

https://www.virtualoffice.com/

Whenever you need to use the office, this option only requires that you book the office room in advance. Additionally, some virtual office might charge a reasonably low monthly fee to the one-time usage fee. This way, you could use them as your business address, and they will collect all your mail.

Another option would be to share an office space with another person. The cost of employing organizational staff and other

the cessation of your laptop's or computer's operations. This is an excellent approach to backing up data.

When it comes to communication, all personal information ought to be sent in an email expressed in code. Doing so reduces the likelihood of the emails to your clients getting diverted by additional unidentified people. You can get this package from service providers such as Hushmail (https://www.hushmail.com/).

Acquire Business Insurance

It can cost you so much time and money when defending yourself from lawsuits and claims filed against you. For this reason, all businesses need to have sufficient insurance coverage.

For your real estate appraisal business, there is at least a couple of insurance coverage that you should be interested in. These are Errors and Omissions (E&O) Insurance and Commercial general liability (CGL).

The Errors and Omissions (E&O) Insurance is the acknowledged liability policy that provides cover from prosecutions linked to errors, oversight or omission in works having to do with appraisals.

Actually, the Board of Real Estate Appraisal in some states, like Colorado, requires home appraisers to take the E&O coverage before they approve you the permit. Several lenders may refrain from ever giving you business if you are working without this insurance.

As for Commercial general liability (CGL) insurance policy, its cover will meet the damages connected to physical harm, personal injury, and damage on the property. It also performs services related to appraisal or injury that occurs on the premises of the business.

Each policy, however, has its own terms and conditions. Different exclusions and deductibles might be spotted in the policies, thus an excellent idea to talk to your insurance agent about your needs first.

Acquire Business Tools

Like any other business, your appraisal firm will require specific equipment and tools to ensure the daily smooth running of the company. Here is a listing of things you should consider acquiring.

Measuring tape for taking measurements outside and inside the properties.

Data Subscription. There are times that you will need information that is essential to your analysis. For instance, comparables, installations, and replacement costs. In this case, some companies provide these data services like:

- PricewaterhouseCoopers (https://www.pwc.com/)

- CompStak (https://compstak.com/)

- Marshall & Swift (https://www.corelogic.com/solutions/marshall-swift.aspx)

- CoStar (https://www.costar.com/)

- MLS (http://www.mls.com/)

Camera. When doing appraisal inspections, you will be required to take photos and include them in the appraisal reports. For this reason, a camera will be quite handy during these times.

There are many good ones for sale at fair prices. Do not rush to get an overly fancy one. However, if you do not have the money to get a camera, you could use a cell phone with an excellent quality pixel camera.

Software. In the appraisal business, you will need some software that assists in writing the appraisal reports and operating the business. You could have a look at software such as:

- Appraisalhost (http://www.appraisalhost.com/)

- Valuelink (https://valuelinksoftware.com/)

- Appraisaldash (https://appraiserdash.com/)

- Anow (https://anow.com/)

- Microsoft Office (https://www.office.com)

Additionally, you will most probably require:

- A laptop

- Safety gear for construction site tours, i.e., helmet, safety boots

- A car

Software Required

Home appraisers, just like everybody else, know very well that time is money. An appraisal software program allows for multiple possibilities to increase efficiency and improvement in productivity.

How can you, therefore, make your appraisal process more efficient and finish more appraisals in a month?

Various software firms provide innovative solutions. Below are a few appraisal software programs worth examining.

TOTAL sketching software
(https://totalstore.alamode.com/product/total-sketch)

TOTAL Sketch and TOTAL Sketch Pro from a la mode by CoreLogic is an efficient sketching software for floor-plans. It can be used on the desktop as well as mobile.

Normally, the regular version is free. However, it is possible to purchase the Pro version to gain more exceptional features that save time. This software includes photometric and Trace mode. It also has free integration with different sketching programs such as Apex and RapidSketch.

These two versions flawlessly blend with the TOTAL system, which facilitates the filling of forms that comprises several shortcuts of data-entry. It also improves your capacity to use comparative sales over and over, as well as open an appraisal over a number of screens.

HomePuter forms processing software
(http://www.homeputer.com/)

HomePuter's Forms Processing Software is a package that includes the newest FHA, Fannie Mae, VA forms, and Freddie Mac. Not only that, but it has AMC-specific and Lender/Client-specific forms.

This software also offers auto-mapping, USPAP addenda, photo imaging, FEMA flood maps, free signature scan, census data, and other innovations. You can also check compliance on it as it provides you with and corrects errors and warnings.

Redstone analytics software
(http://bradfordsoftware.com/redstone/)

Redstone, a Bradford Technologies creation, is a software package that provides appraisers with exceptional analytics. Bradford Technologies maintains that you can attach credible analytics to your report and close your appraisal faster with this appraisal software.

Redstone assists in determining changes, identifying the best comps faster, as well as record the process of selection for comparable sales. It also generates a 1004MC automatically.

ACI analytics software

(http://www.aciweb.com/product/aci-analytics/)

The ACI Analytics desktop collection offers a listing database and analytics to expedite analyses on property cost. The desktop suite comprises of UAD compliance features, sketching software, appraisal delivery, market conditions analysis, and location maps.

There are additional plug-ins for data storage, flood maps, amongst others. According to the company, its settings are highly agreeable with other digital tools. There are two different membership plans offered by the company. One customized for multi -appraiser companies, while the other for sole appraisers.

Anow appraisal management software

(https://anow.com/)

Would you like to well-manage all your clients, orders, fees, and more using a single centralized program? Anow's Appraisal Tracking is the software for you.

In addition, Anow allows numerous foolproof features like financial analytics features calendar, invoicing, map, and email, to ease the improvement of your business planning and workflow.

If online appraisal software is a new thing to you, there are numerous sites online that provide vast information about it.

Appraise-It software suite
(http://www.sfrep.com/products/)

The Appraise-It software suite provides an appraiser with the benefit of having the ability to add signatures, sketches, photos, maps, amongst others. All these can be included in one report. Also, it employs modifications automatically. From sketching to managing pictures and comps to filling of forms, this appraisal software suite provides a vast array of features that save on time.

HouseCanary (https://www.housecanary.com/)

This exceptional software performs precise, swift analytics powered by data. Based online, HouseCanary offers composite appraisals enabled by high-level strategies.

Also, this software's methods are all USPAP standard-compliant. One of its great specialties is that it helps in combination with other third-party software tools. This reduces the cost of operation and also increases speed.

Through merging reports and data, HouseCanary is a reliable tool for appraisal. It can substitute conventional 1004s, BP05, and 2055 systems flawlessly. HouseCanary helps trained home appraisers who work with real estate professionals with immediate results without requests for review.

Moreover, it is flexible as well as versatile. For this reason, this home appraisal software may as well be utilized by several individuals like capital markets operators, lenders, as well as the owners of single-family rental homes.

A la mode (https://www.alamode.com/)

This appraisal software guarantees professional results as it has a variety of capabilities built into it. A la mode can automatically do form-filling, work on Cloud architecture, and improve flood maps. It can also grant you comprehensive analytics as well as gather extensive write-ups for your assessment requirements.

A la mode includes combined software like Vault and Titan Analytics. Therefore, it collects 1004MC records quickly and securely saves your appraisal data. For high-ranking performance, A la mode replies to a number of operational foci such as data entry shortcuts, the capacity to separate appraisal data over several screens, and the reuse of compilations.

For this reason, this software is one of the most common appraisal software at these times. Through the limited trial, you can examine it as a free home appraisal software.

Helpful Apps

I realize that most people in the 21st century rely on tablets and mobile phones. Most of the people I have mentored have resorted to smaller mobile gadgets that are very resourceful in the appraisal practice.

Mobile devices have changed how appraisers administer their services. From sketching plans, taking photos, to making connections with one's team, digital apps have diversified channels to use and make improvements to your process. Below are several apps that appraisers should have. They will be of assistance in taking your plans to the next stage.

Google Drive (https://www.google.com/drive/**)**

This app is one of several distinct cloud storage apps accessible on your tablet or smartphone. It is helpful in sharing reports and data amongst your lenders, homeowners, and the whole team. It is also beneficial for extracting data faster. Any data is accessible, from building plans, property reports, and tax records. Other current apps with comparable usability are Microsoft One Drive and Dropbox.

RapidSketch

(https://apps.apple.com/us/app/rapidsketch/id553876518)

In this app, you will find a tool for diagramming. This tool enables you to draw residential and commercial homes fast and correctly. RapidSketch is especially suitable for the design addendum segment of your Uniform Residential Appraisal Reports. You can use this app for the creation of accurate layouts of a floor plan and measure square footage.

LastPass (https://www.lastpass.com/)

With multiple distinct web logins, it can sometimes be hard to memorize passwords. LastPass allows someone to app passwords in a single location and also save all of the webs. It gives one the ability to log in to web portals belonging to company and real estate firms, information databases, as well as any other websites you may use when doing an appraisal.

Supra e-Key (http://www.supraekey.com)

As an appraiser, there are times that you may arrive at a home and be incapable of access. This could be because of the absence of the homeowner or a door that is locked. With Supra e-Key, home appraisal and real estate professionals can have access to homes by use of a mobile device and a digital keypad. In case the home you are appraising works with the system, download the app, ask for approval, and begin.

Mint (https://www.mint.com/)

In this app, you can follow and oversee the expenses related to the job. A lot of appraisers also use Intuit Quickbooks and Expensify for similar purposes. These apps totally enable you to categorize receipts and take photographs, draft down notes linked to other expenses spent in the business, and also take note of miles driven.

CoPilot GPS (https://copilotgps.com/en-us/)

It is quite a task to find your way to the homes on your list. CoPilot GPS assists you in saving time by generating a path that takes you to every household in the most cost-effective manner. This can either be by distance or time, as per your day's priorities.

Genius Scan (https://thegrizzlylabs.com/genius-scan)

A lot of appraisers love this app as it eases the workload in scanning, uploading, as well as sharing reports via your mobile gadgets. It can even scan and convert handwriting into text. Genius Scan is perfect for producing copies of floor plans, tax records, and many other documents.

Legal Requirements

Like in every other business, there are certain requirements that one ought to have before he or she begins a business. Some of these requirements are mandatory and obligatory by law.

These requirements include:

license. To see your state's required training and register for pocket-friendly online classes, check online for vast information.

One of these sites is McKissock Learning, which allows you to complete coursework on your schedule, thus very flexible. (https://www.mckissock.com/)

Before we dig deeper into the training that you need to become an appraiser, let us first understand exactly why this training is essential to you.

Why go through the long hours of study, coursework, and professional practice?

Well, first and foremost, it will help you be sure of whether that is genuinely what you want to do. It will determine how interested you are in the career and your capacity to do real appraising.

Perhaps you will become much more interested in it, or maybe halfway through the course, you may change your mind. There are eBooks about appraising. However, actual courses will give you more tangible appraising skills as well as do it theoretically by closing case studies.

Also, when you take a course, you may find a supervisory appraiser who may ask you to come back after completing the trainee level courses. These are the minimum level courses and are essential in securing the trainee license.

Normally, it may take two months, depending on your speed and desire to finish the courses. If you do not take the classes, someone else may take your spot, and it may be challenging to secure a place in the future.

In addition, until you have done the courses and received your trainee license, your job experience hours do not count. For this reason, if you stall finding your supervisory appraiser by the time you take the courses, two months' worth of experience hours will be lost. You will have the experience, but the hours will not be officially counted by the board.

Now that we know why the home appraising training is important, let us see exactly what the courses incorporate.

Obtain a Trainee License

For you to become a trainee, you ought to finish specific coursework that presents a solid home appraisal foundation. You not only need to complete but also pass.

There are national course requirements imposed by the Appraiser Qualifications Board (AQB). Some states demand extra coursework. All states require appraisers to begin their career as trainee appraisers, but each state monitors its appraisal industry differently. For specific requirements, verify with your local licensing board.

So, for an appraisal trainee license, a minimum of 75 credit hours comprising appraisal policies, systems, and application is required by the AQB. Also, a four-hour supervisory or trainee class must be done by appraiser trainees.

The requirements for national coursework are:

Basic Appraisal Principles: This coursework takes 30 hours. It opens doors to primary property concepts, legal concerns, business policies, real estate finance, and appraisal principles.

Necessary Appraisal Procedures: This course also takes 30 hours. This course on procedures trains students on the original process of valuation.

In the course, you will find three standard value approaches, i.e., a sales comparison approach, income approach, and cost approach. Methods of data collection, communication of appraisal results, and description of the subject property are also critical subjects in the coursework.

Uniform Standards of Professional Appraisal Practice: In this course, you will take a shorter time than the others as it lasts 15 hours. The USPAP coursework launches the student into the ethical behavior requirements of the industry and the USPAP.

Additionally, you are required to attend a four-hour **administrative trainee class** for 79 hours of the appraisal training. This class was initiated on January 1, 2015. It covers the responsibilities of the trainee and what is expected of them. It also equips one with the skills on mentor relationship and the description of competent performance.

Besides the national course requirements, some states add slightly more time for classwork before becoming an appraiser trainee. Nevertheless, these states still need the four-hour trainee class on top of their distinct state requirements.

Below is a quick outline of a few of these states terms:

- Colorado - 110 hours of coursework

- North Carolina, Tennessee, Kentucky & Georgia - 90 hours of coursework

- New York, California & West Virginia - 150 hours of coursework

- Florida - 100 hours of coursework

Education providers offering approved appraisal courses necessary for a trainee license are not hard to come by. However, they are not formed alike.

For instance, McKissock Learning has had quite an experience in educating real estate professionals. With more than 25 years in existence, the school offers extensive learning that is state-specific. It prepares prospective appraisers to observe integrity and competence in their work.

Real Estate Work Experience

Once you obtain your appraiser trainee license, you can work as a home appraiser only under the mentorship of an accredited home appraiser.

To get your certificate and move to the next level of becoming a licensed home appraiser, you need to finish about 1,000 hours of professional experience. This should be done in no less than 6 months and following the guidance of a licensed home appraiser.

Finding a position as a home appraisal trainee may be challenging. However, you can check out banks, which frequently have the highest need for real estate appraisal services.

You can also find jobs at private appraisal firms. A job at a bank or a place like the American Society of Appraisers can often be very resourceful when at this point in your career. Ensure that you only operate under the mentorship of a certified appraiser. Also, ensure that you keep a track record of the hours you work.

For those just starting out, certified home appraiser Doug Haderie advises that you should "Visit your state board's website and print out the details of each appraiser within a radius of 10 miles and simply start calling them."

College-level Coursework for Appraiser License

After becoming an appraiser trainee and clearing at least 1,000 hours of professional experience under the guidance of a licensed home appraiser, one can finally obtain a license.

Also, some states ask that trainees complete closing introductory coursework or college-level courses or degree programs, like an associate's degree. But, on May 1, 2018, the AQB ceased imposing the national college-level education requirement.

If state appraiser administrative agencies adopt the minimum AQB criteria, then they are good to go. Lots of states do not demand college-level education qualifications. Nevertheless, reach out to your state and confirm the licensing requirements, as well as to inquire if additional coursework is required.

Residential Real Property Appraiser Exam

In some states, you need to complete and pass a real property appraiser exam to become a licensed appraiser. In this exam, you will generally cover statutory considerations, appraisal math, standards of value, real estate business, as well as other subjects required by the state.

To qualify for this exam, it is a general requirement by states that applicants achieve the preceding appraiser trainee requirements. You can find and learn more about your state's examination requirements from your state licensing board.

The Federal Financial Institutions Examination Council has the Appraisal Subcommittee (ASC), which can also be very helpful in learning about your state's appraisal requirements. Contact them and find out.

Submit the Appraiser License Application

Once you complete your required professional experience, meet the educational qualifications, and pass the exam, submit your application for a license. Do this at your state's real estate appraiser's board.

After you have obtained your license, you are free to commence your work as a home appraiser. However, you will still have some restrictions on the kinds of estates you can appraise.

If you yearn for growth in your appraisal business, contemplate renewing your license constantly. This will help you assess more complex properties.

Requirements for state application differ, but commonly include:

Proof of education qualification: Aspirants are usually directed to present the name of the education programs that they have done, the education providers, and the time they completed the program.

Background information: Besides producing social identification information like social security number, candidates are generally required to provide background information. This is with regards to convictions or criminal charges, dismissed or speculated licenses, as well as child support stipulations.

Report on experience: Together with the overall account of your work, you will need to render a statement on your practice in the appraisal industry. The sort of expertise differs by state.

Employment: States ask for a history of jobs to find information on training and also provide confirmation of proper appraisal practice.

Once you become a licensed residential appraiser, you can only appraise noncomplex residential properties that are one to four units. Such property could be worth less than $1 million to $250,000. Additional coursework is needed to appraise more high-value compact homes or estates estimated higher than $1 million.

When you do the additional coursework, you then become a Certified Residential Appraiser.

Becoming a CRA

So exactly how do you become a certified residential appraiser?

Well, for a job as a certified residential appraiser, you must meet the following supplementary qualifications:

All certified residential appraisers are expected to finish AQB-approved appraisal coursework that lasts about 200-plus hours. The earlier coursework is done to acquire your appraisal license matters in the achievement of this goal. Therefore, you have to achieve the credits balance for you to be qualified for the certified appraiser license

As for experience, certified residential appraisers ought to have a minimum of 1,500 hours of professional practice as an appraiser or appraisal trainee. This experience should not be less than 12 months. If you worked as a trainee at some point, the hours of work experience you completed do count toward this total.

For this reason, your obligation would be to make up the balance by working as a licensed appraiser.

In education, the certified residential appraiser's requirements dictate that you need to hold an associate's degree, a total of 30 hours of college-level courses, or a bachelor's degree. You can also do a combination of units, as summarized by The Appraisal Foundation. To comprehend how they are embracing to modern standards and the requirements that you ought to meet them, contact your state's agency.

Once you become a certified residential appraiser, you now have the permission to appraise one to four-unit private structures of any price or complexity. You are also allowed to appraise an undeveloped or vacant property, which is used or best suited for one to four residential units.

If you would like to appraise vacant or unimproved estate befitted for more than four household units, it is necessary that you get extra certifications. You must become a Certified General Appraiser.

Becoming a CGA

Appraisal specialists can further upgrade to certified general appraisers. There are no restrictions on the sort of real estate you can value as a certified general appraiser.

For this certification, the AQB necessitates that an appraiser takes at least one bachelor's degree or higher, or 300 hours of training. Specialists need to also achieve at least fieldwork of no less than 3,000 hours in no fewer than 30 months. In this 3,000 hours, at least 1,500 hours must be spent appraising nonresidential properties.

Online Training Sites

I have come across a few online training platforms that are very helpful and resourceful to a home appraiser. These online training platforms also adhere to the Uniform Standards of Professional Appraisal Practice (USPAP). The USPAP are the regulatory ethics that all home appraisers should abide by, no matter the state of their operation.

Some of these online platforms are:

McKissock Learning. (https://www.mckissock.com) This is generally my topmost choice for home appraiser training. This is because of its extensive geographical accessibility, its offer of an array of courses, as well as outstanding reviews from their customers.

The McKissock Learning platform is a good choice for anybody who needs a manageable learning experience for the licensing, upgrade of licenses, and ongoing training requirements. It is, however, important to note that McKissock Learning does not offer exam prep courses.

OnCourse Learning. (https://www.oncourselearning.com) This platform is a suitable option for home brokers, appraisal companies, and other firms in need of licensing programs for internal appraisers.

If you need appraisal classes for a group of students, Oncourse Learning is the platform for you. Students using it find it exceptionally suitable and easy to use, thus excellent online reviews. If you're a busy professional, do not worry. The courses are also very convenient and flexible. However, like McKissock, OnCourse does not offer exam prep courses.

VanEd. (https://www.vaned.com/) This site is a very good choice for people who have already completed the appraisal training requirements and are about to take an exam. It is good for those who want extra exam preparation. It also has low payment plans and course prices, which professionals in states where VanEd offers pre-licensing courses can take advantage of.

Navigating the platform is very stress-free and efficiently prepares specialists for the appraisal exam. Customer service and course instructors are known to be very helpful and give professionals the guidance that they require.

Relevant Personal Qualities

Organizational skills. Home appraisers ought to have excellent organizational skills to perform all the responsibilities associated with home appraisal well.

Analytical skills. Home appraisers make use of several information references during property appraisal. For this reason, they need to do proper and thorough research, as well as examine all factors before assessing the cost and providing a concluding report in black and white.

Math skills. Rigorously analyzing home residential data incorporates steps like measuring the square footage of the space the building occupies plus the whole estate. Therefore, appraisers must possess high-grade skills in math.

Customer-service skills. Being courteous and respectful is very essential for an appraiser. This is because appraisers interact with clients regularly. Additionally, having such traits may be instrumental in expanding business opportunities in the future.

Time-management skills. Sometimes home appraisers get many properties to appraise in a single day, thus working under time limitations regularly. For this reason, being a good manager of time and meeting deadlines is very relevant.

Problem-solving skills. Unexpected problems may come about when appraising a home's worth. So, you must have the capacity to generate as well as apply the alternative solution. This will help you successfully help you complete the evaluation and report on time.

Business Capital Requirements

An appraisal business is a comparatively economical business to begin. In this business, there is no need for any large appliances, a deluxe vehicle, plenty of employees, or facilities.

You also do not need a place for retail, or other several required costs that absorb money when commencing additional small firms.

You may actually notice that you already have most business properties like a cell phone, computer, a comfortable pair of walking shoes, or a car.

For advice on approaches to reduce and deduct expenses on your income tax form, talk to your accountant.

While it is relatively pocket-friendly, kick-starting your appraisal business entails obtaining several things that are distinct to your vocation.

These items include:

- Appraisal Trainee qualification training, which costs $800 – $1,500 per year.

- Internet fees, MLS access, and cloud storage. This may cost you around $1,000 – $1,500 annually.

- Appraisal software for typing and printing reports, which may cost $2,000 per year.

- A laser mapping tool and other devices. These may cost about $200.

- Omissions and error Insurance with an annual cost of $800 – $1,000.

There are many platforms that you may find assistance in making the right decisions about your capital and how you invest in the business.

You can find this help from financial advisors, other appraisers, or even information online.

Ensure that you get enough information and advice before beginning your business.

How to Grow Your Business

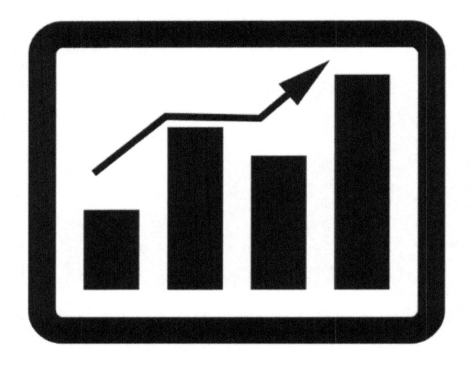

Having an appraisal office and an appraisal firm are two distinct achievements.

An appraisal office normally applies to an individual's shop where he or she works alone to maintain the place.

An appraisal firm, however, usually is an operation that works on a large scale. It has departments of different operations, as well as outlined processes of doing things. Both arrangements work but differently.

Both business decisions are ventures that come with their own collection of advantages and disadvantages. Some business owners' natures favor the one-man appraisal company. They find it a more relaxed and more comfortable way to run things. However, others see growth in a big firm as their most wanted goal.

If you are one of those who desire to grow but need a bit of guidance, here are five steps you can take. These steps have helped many appraisers besides myself, and I believe they may help you too. The measures will place you on a path towards growth. They will push you into this trajectory and not crush you.

Have a Vision

When you aim at building a house, you do not start digging a hole before you have a blueprint

A comprehensive outline of how the ultimate product will look like is very important. Along the way, you may be required to alter the plan. However, you will at least hold a broad view of exactly where you are headed.

Likewise, refrain from beginning the process to your growth without a specific strategy on the way you will move from one point to another. Have an idea of what are you working towards accomplishing, and the reason you are making significant adjustments to the design of your business.

Schedule some time on your calendar when you can take time to be alone and have some real reflection on where you desire your business to grow. When you do so, you will be working on it and not in it. This should be a deliberate move.

You should have both reason and rhyme to your craziness. Have a clear view of what the end looks like before you begin.

Prepare Yourself

After writing and developing your plan, begin setting the groundwork that will make room for growth without constriction. If you have been a solo person running an appraisal shop for several years, it is quite possible that you do not own the modern technology that allows the addition of staff without experiencing some extreme bottlenecks.

- Are you in need of more computer stations?

- Have you considered switching to a server so your current team can operate while moving from one place to another?

- Will your current human resource team operate from the field?

- Do you require to obtain laser measuring devices or tablets for them to work with?

- Do you own the most-recent license capability for your appraisal software?

- Are you in possession of file transfer services like Dropbox, Google Drive, or Onedrive?

- Maybe you need to make systems for your employees to obtain legal entree to the MLS.

Preparations like these need you to think outside the box. If you are used to doing the work alone, it is possible that there various elements that will require prior preparation long before your first call for help advertisement.

Hire for Basics

I have met several appraisers who make the mistake of placing the cart before the horse in their growing process. They turn down too much work, get so busy, and choose to hire a different appraiser to help them at a specific time.

Although it may look like a reasonable step to take, it is too much too soon. Hiring a primary level employee for starters is a more rational course of action to take.

When you get someone to assist with the entry of your data as well as do receptionist services, you may achieve more and free up more of your time than you think. With the extra time you get, you may have the ability to deliver more volumes of work in a day. You could also be better fitted to concentrate on the plan of your business growth. Instead of just letting it grow without direction.

You may also consider hiring more experienced workers who may assist you in being more accurate and cost-effective as an appraiser. This you can do after you ensure that the basics are covered. When you hire an experienced employee, he or she will be able to do the duties that an employee at a beginner's level cannot or should not do.

An individual with a bit more experience and skills might have a lot more to offer to the table. Sketching and in-depth research, regression, and market analysis are all responsibilities that should seemingly be handled before you move to find high-level help.

Hire for Difficult Assignments

After your fundamental and standard levels in human resources are done with, start looking into achieving exceptional development. Most appraisal companies never get to this level.

Could be you are confident and ready for actual growth in your agency bringing in new appraisers. If you are at this stage, move tentatively.

There are several models of business with extra appraisers operating under one firm umbrella. However, every one of them comes with their individual collection of benefits and difficulties.

If you are of gradual and steadfast character, you could train the employees from scratch and help them grow. If you are the sort of person who needs someone helping you as soon as possible, you may need to contemplate selecting a different

Certified Appraiser and present them with benefits that they cannot attain on their own.

Simply examine yourself and find out why an experienced individual would desire to work with you instead of working on their own. If you get an answer to that question, you are most probably able to draw in competent, talented professionals to assist you in growing your venture.

Manage and Review

When you hire someone, you have only taken the first step. After that, you will be required to manage since management is an ongoing process.

At this stage, many appraisal business proprietors conclude that running a 'firm' is not their forte.

Being a manager is not easy because management is a talent that is unique to some temperaments.

Once you make up your mind on growing and hiring, it is necessary that you follow that resolution to the end of the line.

This means that hiring signs you on to the process of managing and training the individuals closely.

There is nothing that drowns a business faster than a relaxed management of employees.

Do not forget that your name is on the line, and the company is your brand.

Marketing Your Business

Consistent marketing is essential to the growth of a business. This is common knowledge for all successful appraisers.

While running your business, there are several marketing techniques for appraisal that you can apply to establish and develop your work.

Outside of appraisal management companies, how can some appraisers generate extra business and fresh contacts? What skills do top appraisers employ to market themselves?

Through my experience and from looking through some leaders in the industry, I acquired some marketing techniques and tips.

In my time, we were less digital. Currently, most appraisers agree that a strong online presence is crucial.

A chain of connections in all of the real estate industry, besides the lending community, is also very essential. These days, the primary approach mostly taken is that your skills in appraisal could be applied in domains that you had never crossed your mind.

Some of these marketing techniques include:

Add some non-lender work into the mix.

A manager and chief appraiser in Hoover, Alabama, once acknowledged that it is getting more difficult for appraisers to create new business by the day. This is mostly due to the power that Appraisal Management Companies exercise.

Sometimes, loan officers are hesitant to work with independent appraisers. Thus, appraisers have found other options and now extend their services to other professionals, accountants, and attorneys. These other professionals may be in need of an appraisal for other reasons besides a loan on a home.

Consider publishing a monthly newsletter.

Like me, several appraisers are folks who are older. For this reason, they are not so conversant with the social media side of things as others may be. Most of them are also not willing to make changes.

Back in the day, door to door was the only marketing tool, and it worked great. My team manages our LinkedIn and Facebook accounts, we also decided to start a newsletter that runs on a monthly basis. So far it has got a rather good reception.

In the newsletter, reports on current trades in our areas of specialty are reported. Also, the changes in zoning and other information we deem valuable is included.

Our articles point out issues about real estate appraisal, as well as a few added details that are particular to us. Things to do with mostly how we offer our services. A newsletter is an easy, affordable, constant method of reaching out to clients.

Also, because the newsletter is published every month, the firm is required to give a little more consideration to marketing the business regularly. This helps avoid overlooking the marketing part of the business when there is heavy appraisal work at the firm.

Since it regularly turns up in people's mailboxes, it serves to limit a situation of feast or famine. We may have customers whose need for an appraisal is only after every one or two years, at least we linger in their minds through the newsletter. Whenever they need an appraiser, they think of us.

It is a very good marketing tool so far. Of course, we no longer do door-to-door marketing, but the newsletter helps us reach out to many people.

Build new relationships.

A research specialist from an Oklahoma-based appraisal company did research and noted that appraisers in the past used to create new market by building relationships with loan officers, sales agents and brokers, developers, mortgage brokers, and title companies.

They maintained their relevance in the real estate industry by joining and attending organizations made up of experts. Some of these organizations include the Appraisal Institute, Mortgage Banking Association, Commercial Real Estate Development Association, CREW, SIOR, CCIM, and MLS.

This has worked well for me, too. Building fresh connections from existing client referrals is a good marketing strategy.

It is key to note that the traditional real estate policy is that the three mysteries to success in the appraisal or any real estate job are 'location, location, and location.' However, I am going to twist that a bit and say that when building a business, the three secrets are 'relationship, relationship, and relationship.'

Several successful appraisers I know usually find opportunities to be heard and grow within the industry. In addition to other services that they offer like substantial valuations of homes, they offer services like giving advice on security valuation of assets for REITS, lenders, and other parties.

They do public speaking and address real estate schools or organizations. They give testimonies in judicial cases and remain updated on issues to do with technology related to the industry, as well as the commercial factors that affect the home appraisal market.

As an appraiser, you can also create new business by giving services in consulting to law firms dealing in real estate. If you choose this area, it is key to note that appraisers with CCIM or MAI classifications are preferred in most cases.

Make your client list diverse.

"Do not put all your eggs in one basket," they say.

This is true in the appraisal business, as well. It is easy to get attached to one or two big customers. This can bring about an unexpected decrease in workflow, especially if the commercial states turn shifts to a direction that is unfavorable for a large Real Estate Investment Trust or lender.

Tough economic times can cause these entities to be fickle. Do not get me wrong. A large REIT or lender as a client base is good for business, but retaining a diverse client account in your core strengths appears like a more fruitful way to grow your market.

You can also use online resources like McKissock. It could be your appraisal wingman. These resources can give you many ideas that you may need for professional development. They have information that could teach you to help create new business and diversify your skills in appraisal.

Distinguish yourself from the competition.

Making your work stand out from the crowd should be the overall aim of your marketing efforts in your appraisal business. This is the most select method of developing a unique and known brand.

While they are key things that represent your brand, a logo or a slogan does not define branding. You need to recognize those things that make your services unique when developing your brand.

To help you with that, you can ask yourself these questions:

- Do I have unique qualifications?

- Is my practice in services that are specific for a particular type of client?

- What do I do to make my services distinct from, and better than other appraisers' services?

- Do I work in a particular geographic zone?

Once you obtain a precise understanding of the competitive advantages you have, you can begin developing a brand that is outstanding in the marketplace.

Create an impressive website.

These days people are inevitably looking for appraiser with an online presence, no matter where you are based.

Developing an up-to-date website that looks professional is very important if you want to grow. This is the heart of your efforts on appraisal marketing in the online platform.

This website does not need to be complicated and costly. You can use a neat design with distinctly written content explaining the activities you do, your way of doing them, as well as the reasons someone should work with you. When building your brand, your website is one of the most valuable tools.

Start a blog.

When your website is finally done, you have the chance to develop your online presence by starting a blog. This is the place where you can assist clients and prospects by sharing your expertise.

Several people are still not sure about the work that appraisers do and the process of appraisal. Demonstrate your knowledge and become the local expert. You will find that people will come to you for answers to their questions.

Make use of online advertising.

Wouldn't it be awesome if your website were on the first page of results when someone does an internet search for an appraiser in your area? Pay-per-click ads are a good investment that can make that happen.

Social media sites can also be good for creating ads. For instance, you want to market to "For Sale By Owners" homeowners, urging them to acquire an appraisal before setting the price for the sale of their home would be good.

Maybe you aspire to target real estate agents. Creating adverts to reach out to those kinds of prospects on social media would be a good idea. Facebook and LinkedIn, for example, provide demographic information that will help your ads reach your target audience.

Hiring the Right Employees

Once you grow big, it is apparent that you will have a tone of work to do.

For this reason, you will need to hire an appraisal assistant.

So exactly how do you go about it?

Step 1: Overcome your fear of hiring.

When it comes to hiring staff, most appraisers are reluctant. But, the advantages of hiring a team exceed the additional task of managing one to a great extent.

You ought to get the right person, put them in the best area, and give them practical training.

Luckily, recent changes in AQB that have already been adopted by some states have made more straightforward the process for new appraisers to get into the field and become fit to operate under your guidance.

Step 2: Search for a suitable candidate.

Post your listing.

It is vital that you acknowledge the abilities you are searching for in a person. If you are looking for an individual with a keen eye for detail to do data entry, or strong organizational abilities to be your receptionist, you will need someone with sharp technological skills.

Unlike past times, post your listing online and skip the print journalism. Steer clear from publications requiring some payment and make use of the free publications.

These can be platforms like your local Labor Department website or Craigslist. Due to the growing dependence on technology in the appraisal world, you need to find applicants who are already using it efficiently.

Filter through the applicants.

Frequently, a job opening posted online is highly likely to have far more applications than you could ever have space for. For this reason, include something in your job posting that requires "hoops" for your applicants to jump through.

Each candidate who fails to follow your precise directions can be disqualified from consideration pronto based on the fact that they were unable to comply with the instructions. This will assist you in evading the reading through of each application.

For instance, demand that individuals that are interested in the job submit a resume and a cover letter to a particular email address. Later, remove any emails that do not bear the two attachments.

There is a high likelihood that you will eliminate around fifty percent of the applicants. After you have filtered your applications to about six or seven, you are ready to move to the next step.

Step 3: Assess your top candidates.

Conduct mini-interviews.

Carrying out an interview for an hour for six or seven candidates is ultimately irrelevant and also consumes a lot of time. Alternatively, plan short interviews that will not take much of your time.

Summon every applicant for a brief interview and a simple computer test. Openly communicate that the interview will take around five minutes.

In the first few minutes of meeting them, you will be able to thoroughly learn about a person's professionalism, promptness, and communication skills. This will help you know if you would like to move forward with the client.

Making a schedule for a brief interview guarantees you will not be forced to sit through a lengthy interview with an individual whom you have instantly realized you do not want to hire.

In the interview, ask a few easy questions like:

- What is your previous work experience?

- Why are you interested in this opportunity?

- Who was your last employer?

Issue a computer test.

If an applicant appears to be an excellent fit with regards to personality, give him or her a simple computer test. This can help you become certain that they do have some of the basic computer skills required to work for you. Watch and keenly follow as they carry out simple tasks such as saving a file and opening an attached document.

Administer a personality profile test.

A personality test very often reveals the details that most applicants can cover throughout an interview. For this reason, consider using a personality profile test like the ones administered by OmniaGroup (https://www.omniagroup.com/). This kind of analysis can be rather expensive, you should consider it as an investment. This is because Omnia offers additional advice on ways to effectively handle this person, in case you hire them.

Conduct a second full-length interview.

After you have reduced your list down to two or three candidates, move on to the next step of conducting a full interview. Often, an applicant will be glad to sit down for a more prolonged talk after the short interview, if you request.

Step 4: Hire your new appraisal assistant.

The 90-day trial.

After finding a candidate, you are willing to work with, hire them on a 90-day based trial. Telling them that it is a trial creates a clear recognition between you and your appraisal assistant that there is no assurance of lasting employment.

Conduct regular employee reviews during this trial period. Ask him or her questions and give feedback on the performance of your assistant. Retain a penned-down record of those reviews for improvement in your future hiring process.

Contract Laborer vs. Employee

Before hiring, figure out if you want to hire a contract laborer or a long-term employee. A contract laborer fills out a W-9 tax form, whereas an employee fills out a W -4 tax form.

The foremost advantage of acquiring a contract laborer instead of an employee is that you will not be required to pay their employee taxes. But, you must comprehend the difference between the two.

For instance, an independent contractor:

- Provides his or her own workspace and equipment

- Sets his or her own work time

- Advertises his or her personal business services

- Works under a free business name

- Has more than one client

Being aware of these differences will determine the way taxes are reserved, as well as shield you from having to pay back penalties and taxes in case of an audit.

Hiring from your home office.

Many appraisers do not feel at ease about hiring employees because they work from a home office and are not comfortable inviting the employees over. A virtual office may be the most suitable option in this case. With the right technology, your employees can work from anywhere in the world.

Paying your appraisal assistant.

If it is possible, paying a contractor on commission is the best option. Since some homes are more complex and need more time, offering a percentage is more reasonable than a flat fee.

Commission them for the work done instead of the time spent. For appraisal trainees, the highest rate you should pay them is 40%. This is if you choose to pay them a flat fee and only in the event of a licensed appraiser assuming full responsibility for the report.

In the exceptional event that an appraiser has done the business on their own, it is paying reasonable to reward them 50%.

Managing an assignment and verifying for correctness usually demands only a tenth of the time it would take to finish if you did on your own.

Set some time to analyze which duties are imminent for you to perform, and which you could delegate to a well-qualified and committed appraisal assistant.

You must keep monitoring the quality of the output of your employees.

Eventually, owning a support staff will relieve you of a lot of work, and you will be able to close more reports and earn more income every year.

As of September 2018, home appraisers earned an average income of $52,600. However, a certified residential home appraiser can make $150,000 plus.

Trainees' earnings range as low as $10,000 annually before taxes, which is considerably less than the other appraisers' earnings. The amount of money an appraiser earns is deeply subject to the appraiser's level of licensing and experience.

Income by Experience Level

Trainee Appraiser

Trainees are compensated with a small payment for every home appraisal that they complete. Fees begin from as low as $50 and rise to $150 as the trainee acquires the skill to accomplish most of the tasks without assistance.

The standard earnings throughout the training phase is a monthly fee of $1,000 to $3,000. Many of the several appraiser trainee positions with a salary are open at state tax assessor's offices or commercial appraisal firms.

A trainee requires at least 1,000 hours of training before passing to take the home appraiser licensing exam.

Home appraisal trainees must conclude a licensing training course and receive a trainee license before being acknowledged for the job.

Potential trainees need to look for a licensed home appraiser who is ready to oversee their work. Several licensed appraisers want trainees to pay a direct fee as reimbursement for the introductory training period. Their supervisor's errors and omissions insurance (E&O) covers the trainees. They are also given admittance to the needed data services.

Residential Appraiser

Licensed appraisers' salaries start from about $35,000 and top out at $80,000. A few management positions sometimes pay more than $100,000.

Appraisers can find work in a lending institution government agency or an appraisal management company (AMC). There are a few positions for field appraisers, most salaried positions are for appraisal reviewers or tax assessors.

Appraisers on an independent fee usually complete most of the appraisals for conforming home equity loan mortgages and refinancing.

For most mortgage appraisals, post-housing emergency fiscal changes need the use of appraisers who are not affiliated with any group. Free appraisers get paid for each job they do.

Jobs from AMCs pay a range of $200 to $350. You can earn a gross income of $50,000 to $100,000 when you make an appraisal daily for 50 weeks.

Certified Residential Appraiser

Certified appraisers can make gross incomes of $75,000 to $200,000. The upper level of earnings goes to appraisers who have regular appraisers working for them, or trainees or live in areas with considerable numbers of high-value homes.

A certified residential appraiser must have at least 1,500 hours of the appraisal practice and pass a particular licensing test. A certified appraiser must complete the appraisal of any home whose value is more than $1 million, or deemed complex.

These measures for complicated appraisals are set by the Uniform Standards of Professional Appraisal Practice (USPAP). Demand is high for certified appraisers. Often, they are required to complete appraisals of any size so that they may be used in legal processes related to tax litigation, divorce, or estate.

Due to the high demand for certified residential appraisers, their charges for their services may be higher than others. The law dictates that appraisers must not base their fees on the cost of a home.

For this reason, they recompense for this stipulation by having a square footage overcharge set to the estimated size. They can range their fee from $500 to $750 or higher.

Though they charge a more-than-average wage, self-reliant appraisers are accountable for all of their investments. A primary E&O system fetches about $1,000 per year.

Data services, software licensing, continuing education, and professional association membership fees cost about $4,000.

In addition to these base expenses, the appraiser is still required to spend on marketing, supplies, workspace, utilities, automobile expenses, and self-employment tax.

Companies doing training courses for appraisers usually paint rosy pictures of high incomes for home appraisers and easy money. In reality, the highest earnings go to individuals who go for long hours working and are skilled at managing their own business. The work done in order to earn such income is also very time-consuming.

Increasing Your Income

There are several ways you can increase your income as an appraiser in the home appraisal industry.

These ways include:

Upgrading your license level.

One of the most significant circumstances influencing the possible revenue for an appraiser is the level of their license. The higher their license level, the more earnings that an appraiser gets.

Ordinarily, a certified residential appraiser makes more than licensed appraisers by $10,000, whereas a certified general appraiser collects almost $18,000 added income than a certified residential appraiser.

Every time you level up, you make a big leap in your annual salary.

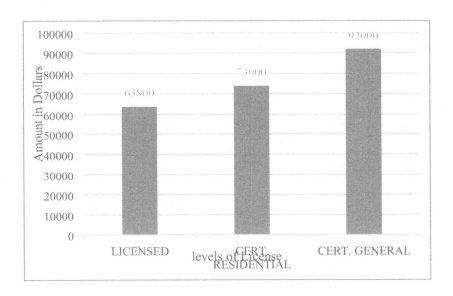

Career Satisfaction

Approximately eight out of ten appraisers are satisfied with their choice of career. A regular job, a strong balance between work and life, plus a decent income are reasons they mention for their satisfaction.

Appraisers who are very content with their vocation make over $47,000 more than appraisers who are not content. This correlation between income and career satisfaction is recognized in all levels of license.

	Average Income	Licensed Appraiser	Certified Res. Appraiser	Certified Gen. Appraiser
Very Content	10200	95650	101525	102598
Content	75100	76875	68894	88526
Neutral	58625	65734	56500	63875
Not Content	53625	54795	46285	47500

The more time an appraiser takes in the profession and takes a small dip approaching the end of their career as they move back on the number of hours worked, the more their average earnings.

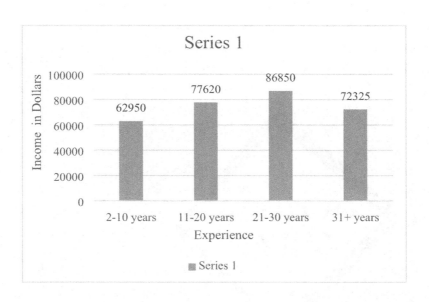

Challenges to Overcome

My experience in the home appraisal industry is a bit similar to the history of the appraisal profession over the last half a decade.

When I was a beginner in the profession, appraisers used to compile appraisals that were of a 2-page handwritten report. These reports consisted of a cost approach, a sketch, physical characteristics, a plat map drawn by hand, a pretty simple comparison sales approach, and one Polaroid picture. A 3 X 5 card printed database was also part of the report and would be published once a week.

These days, appraisals are multi-page articles with heaps of documentation inclusive of highly unique analytics. The reports are in an electronic format that all computer databases can analyze, examine, digest, and question an appraiser's analysis, expertise, and ability to provide a reliable report.

For this reason, it has become increasingly challenging to be an appraiser in the 21st century, unlike my time in the industry. Below are some of the challenges experienced.

Difficulty in Finding a Mentor

Anyone joining the home appraising industry may find it challenging to recruit a mentor. Any appraiser who chooses to be a mentor to a trainee is actually training his or her possible opponent.

For this reason, some appraisers will decline to take on a trainee. Some may choose to only sign off on a share of your experience hours as required by the state.

Others may accept to mentor you, although they will grant you a moderate percentage of the exact fee paid for the task or minimal hourly pay. Once you get a mentor, he or she may actually be a lousy appraiser whose work is sloppy and is not USPAP compliant.

Luckily, ethical supervisory appraisers with excellent work experience and who will give you proper training as well as give you a reasonable pay do exist. But, this may need long and wide networking. You have a significant advantage if you have close friends or family members in the appraisal field.

Long Experience Hours Required

Earlier on, several states fulfilled a condition where for you to obtain a license, you had to reach experience hours in no less than a period of two years after the application date.

For instance, in Ohio, the hours required for licensing or certification (2,000 and 2,500, respectively), has to be obtained in no less than two years. This is even though a standard full-time workweek can end in 2,000 hours in a year.

These experience hours are even higher for certified general appraisers. The AQB, before 1st May 2018, set at least 12 months as the time required to reach the 2,000 hours of experience for licensing.

From the said date, the least is now just six months and 1,000 hours of experience, which is half the time that was required before. An Associates Degree is also no longer needed. Nevertheless, as states take the new AQB changes, many are now embracing the minimum requirements only, thus making this much more comfortable to obtain.

Certified Appraisers Get the Most Work

Many AMCs and larger lenders presently want at least a state-certified appraiser to perform an appraisal. This means that you will not get orders from clients with these conditions if you are only licensed.

An exception could be if a state-certified appraiser investigates the subject home with you and approves the report as your supervisory appraiser. Also, if an order is from a more modest lender with limited strict conditions, you could manage to appraise a property.

Mostly, this applies to larger AMCs and lenders. Therefore, as a licensed appraiser, you should still get some business from more modest credit unions and regional lenders.

Fee Collection and Splitting

You may need an upfront fee in full before you begin working on an appraisal order that you have already accepted directly from a client.

Nevertheless, it may be another issue when a middleman is involved. Usually, an AMC would receive the fees from the client, and then they release your share of funding after you complete the assignment.

Sadly, some firms tend to have a sequence of holding the payment of appraisers.

In fact, there have been actual cases where appraisers had trouble recovering their fees because the middleman company shut down their business. If you have an ample account receivable at those firms, this could bring about a significant monetary loss.

However, these are extreme cases. We do not expect this to happen every day. For this reason, you should get to know more about the company before taking on any appraisal assignments. For instance, find out how long the company has been around and if there has been any past complaints or dispute. If so, find out how they handled it.

Many home appraisers I have talked to complain that middlemen usually take up quite a substantial part of the fees. This is not fair, according to some appraisers, since they are the ones who do most of the work.

The good news is there are many Appraisal Management Companies (AMCs) and firms to choose from. Therefore, if you are not content with one, then you can always find a different company that could accept your terms.

You will definitely need to recognize the support and services that your partnering firm is rendering to you. It is then up to you to make a decision on whether the splitting is fair or not.

Some appraisers that I have spoken to stated that their splitting rate with their AMC ranges from 50% to 70%.

Driving and Weather

You may be required to drive around from time to time, considering the job demands that you go inspect the properties onsite.

Constant driving can be exhausting and could also consume a lot of time. Moreover, the driving may add expenses to your business and decrease the value of your vehicle.

To help in this challenge, some established appraisers concentrate on providing service to a specific region, instead of performing appraisal orders for properties in scattered areas.

Also, to generate a well-written appraisal report, you will be required to check the outside and inside of the subject properties thoroughly. Nevertheless, there are times that the weather could be a problem.

For example, you could be outdoors taking measurements and photos when it is snowing or raining.

This could definitely not be your average day work experience. However, you ought to take the weather condition into account and equip yourself accordingly.

Business Expenses

As you operate an appraisal business, you will be required to pay for the expenses in the business.

Some common expenses include paying for Error and Omission insurance, continuing education, laptop, software subscription, vehicle, license fee, plus other office supplies.

Moreover, you ought to set up your own retirement savings and medical insurance as a self-employed appraiser.

Note that stating these challenges is not meant to deter you from pursuing a career in the home appraisal industry. Instead, it is intended to give you insight into the profession so you can fully equip yourself and make well-versed resolutions.

It can be tough in the beginning, but also quite a rewarding career, once you make it. If you desire to be a home appraiser, do not hesitate to go for it!

Benefits to Reap

Although there are challenges in the home appraisal business, there are many benefits to starting a business in the industry. While it has challenges, home appraising has advantages that anyone pursuing a new business would desire.

Strong Demand

Appraisals are usually needed in several real-life situations. For instance, refinancing, divorce estate settlement, and home purchasing or selling. In these scenarios, your appraisal expertise would be required.

Lately, there is a substantial deficit of home appraisers over various states.

Some states like Kentucky have very few appraisers per 1,000 workers. West Virginia already has the most concentrated number of appraisers, it is still a low ratio of appraisers to workers.

Control Over Schedule

Your work will be according to the plan assigned by your company if you are an employee paid on a salary basis. But, if you are a self-employed appraiser, then you may have more considerable power over your work plan.

To accommodate their client's schedule, some other self-employed experts have a higher opportunity of meeting them after regular office times or throughout the weekend.

Otherwise, your appraisal could be one of the most significant elements in concluding whether a home deal can go through or not. For this reason, most people are ready to plan a visit to the property, depending on your availability.

Many real estate agents will work at fitting to your schedule and stroll through the home with you, even if the seller is not accessible at your inquired time. After all, they have a tremendous motivation to get the process moving cold as smooth as possible.

Independent Working Time

While you will get the opportunity to meet several real estate sales associates and homeowners, you may also relish some time accomplishing tasks alone.

Appraisal work often does not need collaboration with another person, so you will be lucky to work alone when you want. You would be free to spend a requisite amount of time operating freely, carrying out research, interpreting data, and drafting appraisal reports.

Variety of Appraisal Niches

The overall populace frequently has a misconception that appraisers only work on regular assignments like average residential houses, yet, this career has a lot more to offer. If you would like, you could also appraise other things like hotels, office buildings, farms, golf courses, or other types of compound assets.

You may also concentrate your work on lawsuit appraisal, relocation appraisal, survey appraisal, plus many others.

In fact, several appraisers who wish to become experts in a specialized niche usually head to higher earnings. That is because it would need years of practice to acquire such advanced knowledge, which makes it hard to be replaced by your competitors.

Non-Sales Oriented

Nothing is wrong with a sales job. However, it is just not meant for everybody.

You may consume a lot of time serving and convincing a client to buy a product. However, if you do not make a sale, you will not receive your payment.

However, when you take on a task as an appraiser, you will still get your payment despite your client agreeing with your appraisal or not.

Great Potential in Earning

The average salary of home appraisers, according to the Bureau of Labor Statistics, is $54,010 per year.

If you achieve the Certified General Appraiser license and dedicate yourself to a certain niche, your income potential could be even more rewarding.

Dynamic Working Lifestyle

Some people hate the idea of working in a permanent office set throughout the year. They usually prefer a number of new developments in their work setting.

As a home appraiser, you will not be held to an office desk the whole time because you will be moving from one place to another inspecting homes.

You will get to visit and pick up information about diverse localities, and also get to see different varieties of real estate.

Conclusion

As you have seen by now, home appraising is a business that you can easily venture into. It is flexible and can earn you a good income.

When you grow, you can also mentor other upcoming appraisers and help them acquire the skills to earn a substantial income.

Like any other business, you will most definitely go through challenges, especially at the beginning of your journey in this career. However, you should not give up. Instead, put on a good fight and aim for growth.

Patience is key in this process as it does not grow in a short span of time. With patience, hard work, constant upgrading, and good marketing skills, success is guaranteed.

If this book has helped you in any way, would you please consider leaving a review where ever you purchased this book? I would sincerely appreciate it.

Best wishes in your new business endeavors!

Made in the USA
Las Vegas, NV
27 June 2022

50801419R00069